Original title:
Lush Lyrics

Copyright © 2025 Creative Arts Management OÜ
All rights reserved.

Author: Adrian Caldwell
ISBN HARDBACK: 978-1-80567-050-6
ISBN PAPERBACK: 978-1-80567-130-5

The Call of the Wild

The owl hoots loud, a silly request,
The raccoon winks, it's such a jest.
A bear in a tutu, dancing away,
In the land of the wild, it's party day!

The squirrels are gossiping, tails in a twist,
As birds on a branch can't resist the list.
With laughter that echoes, the trees join in,
A raucous affair where nonsense can win.

Imagery in the Meadow

In the meadow, frogs wear crowns of gold,
While daisies whisper secrets untold.
A butterfly stumbles, its wings in a tangle,
And giggles erupt where grasses dangle.

Chasing the shadows, a rabbit does hop,
With a silly dance, it won't ever stop.
The flowers all chuckle, their colors so bright,
In this meadow of laughter, all feels just right.

Flourish and Fable

Once there was a tree with a grin so wide,
It tickled the leaves, made the branches slide.
A squirrel, astonished, let out a squeak,
As laughter rumbled from the root to the peak.

Down by the stream, a fish tried to sing,
With bubbles of giggles that made the day spring.
A turtle rolled over, laughing in glee,
In this world of tales, all wild and free.

Traces of Twilight

The sun dips low with a yawning sigh,
As fireflies wink, oh-so-spry.
A raccoon in sneakers is running for fun,
In this twilight stage, all fables spun.

The moon hangs bright, a giant cheese wheel,
As stars play tag, with an electric feel.
In the traces of evening, laughter ignites,
Beneath the dark sky, all frolics and flights.

Harmonies of the Heart

In the symphony of lunch, a feast,
Pasta sings, while salad's a beast.
Bananas waltz in a fruity parade,
Muffins stand guard, unafraid.

Burgers play drums, with sass and flair,
Dancing picks up crumbs from the air.
Cupcakes giggle with frosting delight,
As pickles take center stage, what a sight!

Canvas of the Sky

Clouds brush strokes of silly green,
Sunwalkers wear shades, oh how keen!
Rainbows creep in with giggles profound,
While thunder's a jester with a rumbling sound.

Kites fly high in a wobbly style,
They flirt with the birds, crack a smile.
The moon winks down, pulling the strings,
While stars play tag, oh what fun things!

The Dance of Daisies

Daisies sashay in fields of grace,
Sneezing tulips join in the race.
Butterflies giggle, spinning around,
While crickets keep time with a chirpy sound.

Sunflowers twirl in yellow delight,
Against the backdrop of a glorious sight.
Bees buzz a tune that's sweet as pie,
As daisies declare, "We'll dance till we die!"

Aromas of the Earth

The bakery's warmth hugs you like a friend,
While coffee beans giggle, their aroma will blend.
Garlic and herbs spark a savory fight,
They swirl through the air like a savory kite.

Fresh-cut grass whispers a tropical song,
While cinnamon swirls weave in all along.
Petunias perfume the most funny affair,
Mouth watering scents fill the joyful air!

Echoes of Nature's Muse

In the forest, a squirrel sings,
Twirling around like he's got wings.
A raccoon winks with a cheeky grin,
As if the tree tops are where he's been.

The owls hoot with a wink of night,
Dancing shadows give such delight.
While frogs croak their own serenade,
In this wild world, no plans are made.

Vibrant Verses

Bees buzzing like tiny drums,
They laugh as they dodge all the slums.
Flowers prance, wearing bright hues,
As the sun dresses in golden views.

A snail slips by, slow on his quest,
Claiming the title of nature's best.
His shell shimmers with a wink and tease,
While ants march on with utmost ease.

Blooming with Emotion

Petunias gossip, a flowery crew,
Whispering secrets in morning dew.
Daisies giggle, each with a wish,
While a crow caws, planning a dish.

Oh, the tulips sway, giving high fives,
While jolly bees craft their buzzing jives.
A butterfly floats, dressed to impress,
Life's a carnival, and nothing's a mess.

Chants of the Wildflowers

Margaret the daffodil struts so bold,
In a garden full of stories untold.
Sunflowers nod, relishing the breeze,
While thistles chuckle, teasing the trees.

Lilies dive into the pond's embrace,
With frogs in tuxedos, they leap in grace.
Nature's a theater, a laughter fest,
Combining colors, we are truly blessed.

Songs from the Canopy

Up in the trees, the birds take flight,
Chirping tunes through day and night.
A squirrel dances while the pitch is high,
Swinging his tail, oh me, oh my!

Branches sway in a gentle cheer,
Raccoons gather, munching on a pear.
The wise old owl sleeps through the noise,
Dreaming of mischief with his feathery boys.

Sunlight trickles in, truly divine,
Flavors of berries on branches align.
The melody plays, the leaves do hum,
Nature's orchestra, what a fun drum!

Laughter echoes through the green abyss,
Even a turtle feels the bliss.
They all join in for a leafy brawl,
Singing their songs, oh, have a ball!

Cascade of Colors

Petals drop like a painter's brush,
In shades of pink and a vibrant crush.
Bees buzz by, with a silly posture,
Sharing nectar like they're on a rapture.

Tulips giggle in the morning light,
Making daisies blush, oh, what a sight!
Caterpillars join, wearing tiny hats,
Pretending to dance like the acrobats.

Rainbows spill from above so grand,
Flowers sway, taking a stand.
A playful breeze shakes all around,
Nature's laughter is an uproarious sound.

The honey-drip flavor, oh so sweet,
Even the lightning bugs tap their feet.
In this garden, color's the name,
Every bloom playing a funny game!

Poetry in Petal Form

Roses recite with a playful grin,
While tulips argue who'll dance and spin.
Sunflowers chuckle high above,
Whispering secrets of plant-based love.

Daisies tease with their wide open eyes,
Trying to impress all the passing flies.
Lilies float in a pond so blue,
Giggling gently, saying, "Look at you!"

Petals fall with a tip and tap,
Frogs join in for a ribbit clap.
Each bloom sings a quirky rhyme,
In this garden, laughter bides its time.

Nature's lyrics fill the air,
Quirky melodies everywhere.
Amidst the petals, joy takes flight,
Making the world feel warm and bright!

Serenade to the Silent Grove

In a grove where the maples groan,
Trees whisper secrets, all alone.
A raccoon sneezes, causing a stir,
Owls turn their heads, saying, "Oh, pure!"

Frogs croak softly, a tuneful jest,
Their chorus brings a humorous quest.
Squirrels shout, holding acorn praise,
Debating loudly on how to amaze.

The sun dips low, painting skies ablaze,
While shadows dance in whimsical ways.
Every twig creaks a laughter's key,
Creating rhythms as wild as can be.

So join the grove, with mirth and cheer,
Echoes of chuckles you're sure to hear.
In this sanctuary, humor glows,
Nature's serenade forever flows!

Verdant Whispers

The grass is always greener,
But mine is full of weeds.
The flowers tell me secrets,
Like how to plant misdeeds.

Bumblebees with buzzing tales,
They laugh at my odd shoe.
I dance like I'm a tree branch,
But I'm a giant kangaroo.

The sun plays peek-a-boo,
From behind the leafy crowns.
I trip over my laces,
In these silly, leafy towns.

With every tumble I take,
The daisies crack a grin.
They say, 'Don't sweat the petals,
Just let the fun begin!'

Serenade of the Green

Oh, watch the ferns do ballet,
While squirrels sing in key.
The leaves are great musicians,
When they fall right on me.

The garden hose is frantic,
Spraying water up high.
It's a water park adventure—
Who knew it'd make me fly?

With every potato planted,
I wear a goofy hat.
The worms are my committee,
And my dance partner's a cat.

So here's to plants and laughter,
To petals soft and bright.
Let's serenade the garden,
With jokes that feel just right!

The Blooming Echo

When flowers start their giggle,
The tulips join the fun.
A daisy throws confetti,
Wishing autumn has run.

The daisies talk about me,
In whispers sweet and sly.
They say I have two left feet,
But I still give it a try.

My carrots get to chatting,
In their cozy, crinkled way.
They share the gossip of potatoes,
While I'm dancing in the hay.

Every bloom's a comedy,
Nature's silly feast.
With petals tossed like popcorn,
I'll laugh until I'm leased!

Rhythms of the Meadow

A meadow full of jiggles,
Where flowers do the twist.
The bunnies hop in rhythm,
Oh, how could we resist?

The grasshoppers are DJing,
As crickets tap their feet.
Listen close to their music,
It's a hopping, bouncing beat.

I twirl and twist with daisies,
In this green and grassy scene.
A silly dance of nature,
It's the best that you've ever seen.

So join the meadow party,
With laughter intertwined.
We'll sway among the blossoms,
Let's leave all worries behind!

The Swaying Silhouettes

In the dusk, the shadows dance,
Beneath the trees, they take a chance.
With every sway, a giggle breaks,
Nature's puppets, in silly shakes.

Frogs croak tunes, a comical choir,
Each note a leap, they never tire.
Crickets chirp in a funny beat,
While fireflies twirl on tiny feet.

The breeze joins in, a shaking hand,
As grasshoppers hop, they form a band.
With antics bright, the night feels grand,
Under the stars, it's all a planned.

So let's all sway like silly fools,
Join the fun, let's break the rules.
In this show of shadows and light,
We find the joy of nature's night.

Nature's Choral Canvas

Birds in trees, a feathery crew,
Singing songs that sound askew.
With twirls and hops, they share their cheer,
Each note a laugh, so loud and clear.

Flowers bloom with colors bright,
In the breeze, they dance in delight.
Bees buzz along, a bumbling tune,
While ants march off, a comical platoon.

Clouds float by, they're puffed with pride,
Like fluffy pillows, they glide and slide.
Yet raindrops fall, a splat, a joke,
Splashing mud on a dancing bloke.

Nature's art, both wild and free,
A chorus sprouting, just wait and see.
Each leaf a brushstroke, a funny quirk,
In this canvas, where we all smirk.

Where the Wild Things Sing

Out in the woods, where laughter blossoms,
Creatures cavort—this place is awesome!
Squirrels chatter with witty remarks,
While raccoons dance under the sparks.

The owls hoot in a wise disguise,
With comical winks and knowing eyes.
Wandering foxes play hide-and-seek,
While hedgehogs puff, so cute and meek.

In a glade, the wild things meet,
To share their tales and frolic sweet.
Each one a clown in nature's show,
With antics grand, they steal the glow.

Where the wild things sing, join the fun,
Laughter echoing, we're never done.
In this wild world, we find our way,
Chasing joy, come join the play!

Cradled in Canopy

Wrapped in leaves, where giggles grow,
The branches sway, putting on a show.
With whispers soft, the wind does tease,
As squirrels leap with comic ease.

In the canopy, a party brews,
With dappled light in different hues.
Each sunbeam tickles, igniting glee,
Leaves giggle softly in harmony.

Beneath the boughs, a secret plot,
Where mischief brews and laughter's caught.
A band of critters, they play their part,
Nature's jesters with wild heart.

So come and join this leafy spree,
Cradled in green, happy and free.
With laughter echoing through the trees,
Together we'll dance with the gentle breeze.

Jewels of the Forest

In the woods, a squirrel prances,
With acorns bouncing on his chances.
A berry bush wears jeweled hats,
Sipping sunshine, chatting with the chats.

The mushrooms giggle, round and bright,
Their polka-dot tops a silly sight.
A raccoon dances, tail all fluffed,
While chipmunks giggle, feeling rough and tough.

Leaves are laughing in playful tease,
As nature plays a game with ease.
The forest sings a quirky song,
Where every creature feels they belong.

What treasures dwell in greens and browns?
With nature's jesters, never frowns.
Each nook and cranny, a joyful jest,
In this leafy realm, life is the best!

Brushing Up Against the Breeze

A dandelion dreams of blowing high,
With whispers of wind, it's flying by.
Tickled leaves sway in giddy spins,
As the breeze invites the fun to begin.

The butterflies boast of bright ballet,
While bees hum tunes that sway and play.
Grass blade wiggles, trying to dance,
In this soft air, there's nothing by chance.

The clouds snicker, taking their time,
Floating above like a goofy rhyme.
A picnic spread, so wild and carefree,
With ants having parties, a sight to see!

In the arms of the wind, all's a tease,
Where laughter dances, brushing the trees.
Each gust a giggle, each swirl a cheer,
In this breezy world, the fun's so near.

Layered Landscapes

Mountains piled high, a rocky stack,
With pebbles arguing, none look back.
The fields below wear laughter's glow,
While the streams slip by, putting on a show.

Clouds wearing pajamas float low and wide,
As the hills giggle, swaying with pride.
Rivers do loop-de-loops in the sun,
While crickets play music, having some fun.

A valley of flowers starts a parade,
With petals all bright, a colorful charade.
But watch out for bees in a comical rush,
Wearing tiny hats, they're in a big hush!

Layered marvels in nature's embrace,
Funny sights packed in this vibrant space.
With every curve, a story unfolds,
In this landscape of laughs, all laughter behold!

Embracing the Wild

In the wild, where whimsy roams,
Creatures play in nature's homes.
Raccoons wearing masks, oh what a show,
While the frogs practice their croaky glow.

Bushes gossip about the sneaky hare,
As butterflies flutter, combing their hair.
A chorus of crickets with voices so fine,
Chanting verses to weave a line.

Trees with arms wide open, embrace the fun,
Hoisting owls hooting, 'come join the sun!'
The grass below quakes with giggly smells,
As ants march on, ringing their bells.

In this wild embrace, laughter ignites,
Where every creature finds joy in sights.
Embracing the chaos, with twirls and swirls,
In nature's charade, the wild sparkles and twirls!

Whispers of the Woodland

In the trees, the squirrels chatter,
A debate on the best kind of batter.
Mushrooms dance in polka dots,
While wise old owls plot silly plots.

Frogs croak jazz beneath the moon,
While fireflies blink, "We'll be there soon!"
The grass tickles as rabbits leap,
In a ballet that would wake the sheep.

Ticks and tocks of nature's clock,
A picnic planned on the old rock.
Ants serve tea with acorn cups,
As caterpillars dance with hiccups.

The wind joins in with a cheeky grin,
A tickle fight that's sure to win.
All is merry, the world's a show,
In woodland whispers, fun will flow.

Essence of Eden

In a garden where bees don tuxedos,
Dancing wildly to sweet staccatos.
Tomatoes wear sunglasses so bright,
While carrots break out in disco light.

A cucumber cracks jokes 'bout sour faces,
While flowers strut in towering graces.
Apples giggle on branches so free,
Sharing secrets with buzzing honeybees.

The soil hums with a tickling tune,
While veggies dream of a cartoon moon.
Pumpkins chuckle, their gourd hearts swell,
Halloween jokes, they'd love to tell.

With rainbows draping across the sky,
Every giggle makes the rabbits fly.
In this Eden, laughter's the key,
Nature's fun fest, forever carefree.

Rhapsody of the Roots

Roots are jiving down below,
With worms in disco, putting on a show.
Nuts are gossiping, oh so grand,
As they shuffle their acorn band.

Earthworms wiggle to the beat,
As mushrooms tap their tiny feet.
A beetle sips on morning dew,
While singing tunes that are rather new.

Tangled tales beneath our feet,
With every twist, a new heartbeat.
Bringing laughter to the blooms,
While the soil fills the rooms.

In a rhapsody of roots below,
Nature's giggles start to grow.
Underneath in a world so bold,
Every story worth its weight in gold.

Blooming Inspirations

Petals flutter in the springtime breeze,
They giggle softly, "Can we be these?"
Daisies hold hands in a flower chain,
While tulips joke 'bout a pollen rain.

Worms pass notes, a secret plan,
To throw a party as quick as they can.
With tiny hats and striped balloons,
They dance beneath the silvery moons.

Each bud bursts with dreams and play,
Shouting, "Hooray for a sunny day!"
Chasing shadows with playful glee,
Through blooming paths, so wild and free.

Inspirations rise from earthy cheer,
Every blossom whispers, "Join us here!"
In this garden where laughter ignites,
Nature's joy sparkles in delight.

Seeking Solace in Green

In a forest where squirrels dance,
I tripped over my own two feet.
They laughed and cheered, a raucous glance,
As my dignity faced defeat.

Frogs croak jokes with ribbiting glee,
As leaves whisper secrets, quite absurd.
I chuckle, sip my wildflower tea,
Nature's humor is ever heard.

Heartstrings in the Harvest

At a pumpkin patch, I find my fate,
Big gourds look like they've missed gym day.
I pose with pride, oh, how I celebrate,
    While half of them just roll away.

Cornstalks sway to their own wide tune,
As scarecrows strike a comical pose.
I laugh so hard, I swoon,
    Nature's antics, I suppose.

Intricate Interludes

A butterfly flits in a dizzy flight,
Dandelions giggle in the breeze.
I chase them, what a silly sight,
While buzzing bees buzz with such ease.

The trees gossip in rustling cheer,
Flowers bloom just to tease my shoes.
I stumble on roots they hide with leer,
Nature's jokes are hard to refuse.

Nature's Heartfelt Bequest

A chipmunk stole my sandwich slice,
With a grin and a dash, he was gone.
I can't help but laugh at the price,
Nature's jesters embrace the dawn.

Raindrops dance on my upturned face,
They tickle and tease with their own flair.
In every drop, there's a funny grace,
Nature's gift, if you dare to care.

Dances with the Dandelions

In the breeze, they spin and twirl,
Little dancers in a swirl.
With their golden heads held high,
They wink at clouds that drift on by.

Tickle your nose, they start to sneeze,
Those tiny seeds float with such ease.
I chase them down, they tease my feet,
"Catch us if you can!" they say with glee.

Their fluff's a crown on my wild hair,
A royal look, in sunlit air.
With every sneeze, I laugh and clap,
Nature's jesters in a snap!

A dance-off with a bumblebee,
Who hops and buzzes playfully.
Together, we create a song,
With giggles, we just can't go wrong.

Scents of the Wildflowers

In fields of colors bright and bold,
The flowers whisper secrets old.
A daisy winks, a tulip sighs,
While poppies play at hide and spies.

Oh, what a smell! A fragrant joke,
The daisies giggle, the roses poke.
"Guess my scent!" chirps lavender,
While sunflowers laugh and nod, "For sure!"

The bees compose a buzzing tune,
To serenade the afternoon.
I trip on blooms, a silly fall,
With wildflowers they laugh, enthralled!

Their colors blend, like paint in streams,
Each bloom's a burst of sunny dreams.
In this garden, joy's hard to hide,
With wildflowers, life's a funny ride!

An Ode to Overgrowth

A jungle of leaves, so wildly sprawled,
Where garden gnomes look mildly appalled.
With vines that twist in every way,
It seems like nature loves to play.

The hedges laugh, they rise and fall,
As if to say, "We've got it all!"
A tangle dance, a clumsy prance,
In the overgrowth, we take a chance.

The weeds have formed a rebel band,
While flowers sigh, "Please take a stand!"
Together, they plot a playful strife,
Anarchy in plant life, oh what a life!

A squirrel, a thief of seeds and nuts,
Performs a show, he's showing guts.
With leafy crowns, the plants all cheer,
In chaos, the laughter's loud and clear!

Symphony of the Wild

In the forest, squirrels play,
Chasing shadows, on a spree.
Frogs croak loud, they've got something to say,
While birds sing tunes of glee.

The raccoons waltz on the hill,
With a swagger that's quite absurd.
A parade of giggles, all for the thrill,
Nature's chorus without a word.

Bunnies hop to a funky beat,
With cotton tails bouncing high.
Their little dance can't be beat,
As they twirl beneath the sky.

A bear takes a break for a snack,
Juggling berries, oh what a sight!
Singing loud with a funny crack,
In this wild jam, all feels right.

Petals in the Breeze

Daisies nod, a funny crew,
Telling jokes without a care.
Butterflies in tutus too,
Flutter with a flair to share.

The sunflowers wear big hats,
As they sway to a soft tune.
Chatting sweetly with the rats,
Underneath the bright, warm moon.

Tulips gossip, make a plan,
To prank the clumsy bumblebee.
"Watch him trip, that goofy man!"
Petals laugh, wild and free.

When the wind begins to swirl,
They twist and curl in crazy spins.
Petals dance, the story unfurls,
A garden bursting with grins.

Harmonies of the Heartland

In fields where the corn does grow,
Dance of critters, near and far.
Chickens cluck with a comic flow,
As the cows laugh from afar.

The pigs are pro with their jive,
Rolling around in the mud.
While the sheep are quite alive,
With woolly antics that are stud.

Roosters crow with silly flair,
Trying to steal the spotlight bright.
While the goats climb high in the air,
Chasing clouds, what a delightful sight!

This farm's not shy to create,
Tunes of whimsy, all age-long.
When laughter mixes with their fate,
You'll find them all singing along.

The Dance of Sunlit Leaves

Leaves are twirling in delight,
Dancing shadows on the ground.
They spin around, a joyful sight,
As sunlight glimmers, all around.

The acorns giggle, take their spin,
Rolling down with laughter loud.
A big oak tree joins in, oh what a grin,
Caught up in the nature crowd.

Squirrels bust a move so cool,
Doing flips with lots of style.
Nature's groove, an endless school,
Making us chuckle all the while.

Whispers in the wind do play,
Each leaf has mischief in their core.
A funny show, all through the day,
Nature's dance forevermore.

Verses Beneath the Boughs

Underneath the bending trees,
A squirrel plays with the bees.
He dances odd, quite like a fool,
While birds chirp loud, breaking the rule.

The sun peeks through in golden beams,
Tickling the leaves, igniting dreams.
The grass is soft, a vibrant mat,
With ants parading, all in a chat.

Stray cats nap beneath the shade,
While I'm lost in this leafy parade.
A chorus of laughter fills the air,
As branches sway without a care.

Nature giggles, it's quite absurd,
As trees gossip, not a word unheard.
In this place where silliness reigns,
I'll stay forever, free from chains.

Poetic Blooming in Soft Shadows.

In gardens where the roses play,
A bumblebee flew the wrong way.
He buzzed by blooms, too big to miss,
And crashed right in—oh sweet bee bliss!

The daisies giggle, petals shake,
As tulips whisper of a mistake.
They point and laugh, it's quite a scene,
Nature's humor is so serene.

While butterflies hold court on leaves,
A caterpillar laughs and grieves.
He wished for wings, that's what he said,
But ended up on a garden bed!

Time trudges on, the sun pops free,
While shadows dance around with glee.
A world of joy, a sight to behold,
In soft shadows where mischief unfolds.

Whispers of Verdant Dreams

In the glade where ferns do sway,
I heard a frog croak, "It's my day!"
He leaps and lands with splashes loud,
With a princely pose, he's quite proud.

The trees conspire, whisper and nod,
While pink flamingos play at God.
Strutting their stuff with pure delight,
In this green world, all feels right.

A hedgehog rolls in a spiky ball,
Chasing shadows, he's having a ball.
"Oh dear me!" he shouts with cheer,
"I'm the fastest, come see me here!"

But nature giggles, a twist takes flight,
As he bumps a squirrel and makes it right.
Together they romp under the sun,
In whispers of dreams, they both had fun.

Melodies in Bloom

Oh, the daisies sing with joy,
A tiny rabbit, just a boy.
He hops along with rhythmic grace,
Chasing butterflies in a race.

The daisies tease the bumblebee,
"Why buzz with such haste? Just see!"
The bee just laughs, can't waste a beat,
In this wild dance, he finds his seat.

A turtle joins, slow and wise,
Excited laughter fills the skies.
He's got the moves, in his own way,
While bunnies leap like they're on display.

In kaleidoscopes of vivid hues,
The garden swirls in joyful news.
A quirky tune plays clear and bright,
Melodies bloom in pure delight.

Symphony of the Evergreen

In the forest, trees sway,
Dancing to the wind's play.
Squirrels juggling acorns round,
Nature's laughter is profound.

Bunnies hop, then stop to stare,
Barking dogs give quite a scare.
Frogs croak out a silly rhyme,
Chirping birds keep perfect time.

Mice in boots tap on the ground,
Hands in pockets, they're quite profound.
Rabbits wear their best attire,
For this musical that won't expire.

Deep Roots, High Hopes

Roots run deep, but what a sight,
Crickets chirp to keep it bright.
Worms in tuxedos, oh so neat,
Twist and shout to that funky beat.

Up above, the flowers sway,
Telling jokes that make them play.
Bees in shades buzz with delight,
Planning parties every night.

Succulents stretch and swing around,
Their partners lost, but that's profound.
Potatoes wear a grumpy frown,
Yet humor grows beneath the ground.

The Garden of Unspoken Words

In the garden where secrets lie,
Beans in boots all wonder why.
Tomatoes blushing, red on vine,
Whispering thoughts with a twist of twine.

Cornfields giggle, tall and bright,
Making friends with stars at night.
Pumpkins grinning, sharing tales,
Of ghostly ships and whispering sails.

Bees exchange the latest buzz,
While daisies argue just because.
In this space where silence sings,
Every plant has funny things.

Harmonious Fragrance

Flowers fight for perfume crown,
Roses tease and lilies frown.
Daisies tickle with a wink,
Sniffing chaos, who would think?

Lavender giggles, setting the scene,
While mint leaves practice their routine.
Jasmine spills jokes on the breeze,
Spreading laughter with such ease.

In this harmony of scents,
Rascally roots hold the suspense.
A fragrant giggle fills the air,
Nature's jesters everywhere!

Nature's Sonnet

In the garden, worms dance with glee,
Sipping on dew like it's fancy tea.
Blades of grass tickle my toes,
While squirrels argue over their woes.

A snail moves at a hilarious pace,
With a shell that's a funny old case.
Flowers gossip, petals all aflutter,
Telling tales of the neighborhood's clutter.

Bees wear shades, buzzing so proud,
Making sweet tunes, attracting a crowd.
Nature's jesters, all in a row,
Performing a show that's quite the blow.

So let's laugh as the crickets sing,
And let our hearts take flight on a wing.
For in this chaos, joy does reside,
In a world where nature takes us for a ride.

Petals of the Wind

Whispers of blooms above my head,
Gossiping petals that won't stay wed.
They float and twirl, a colorful spree,
Making grassy hats for the bees with glee.

Dandelions puff like fluffy clowns,
While tulips wear the boldest crowns.
With laughter carried on the breeze,
They tickle the noses of passing leaves.

A butterfly flits, oh what a tease,
Chasing its shadow with utmost ease.
While sunflowers grin, tall and grand,
Holding secrets of this funny land.

So let's dance with the petals around,
Lost in the humor that's joyfully found.
For nature's comedy is the best of all,
As we laugh and twirl to the floral call.

The Song of the Seasons

Spring's a prankster with blossomed pranks,
Puddles splash, giving boots some shanks.
Flowers poke heads through the snow,
As winter sulks, 'cause it's time to go.

Summer's a joker, tossing shade,
Ice cream drips, a sticky charade.
Sizzling laughs from the beach goers,
With flip-flops flapping, joy's roaring roars.

Autumn chuckles, leaves in a spin,
A game of sweep, where the fun begins.
Sweaters hug close, while the air gets brisk,
And pumpkins grin, giving 'gourd' a twist.

Winter's a prankster, hoarding the cold,
Snowmen emerge, their stories retold.
With mittens so floppy, let the games start,
As seasons unite in a comical heart.

Under the Canopy of Stars

Beneath the stars, so brightly they twinkle,
The moon's silver spoon serves cosmic crinkle.
Owls hoot jokes while the crickets beat,
Making a symphony that's oh-so-sweet.

Fireflies flicker, dancing in line,
Like tiny lights at a quirky design.
With giggles released in the cool night air,
They play hide and seek without a care.

The clouds drift softly, painting delight,
Whispering secrets to the laughing night.
Stars plot to tickle the dreaming trees,
As night wraps us in its joyful pleas.

Let's revel under this sparkling stage,
Finding fun in the cosmic page.
So take a breath and let laughter soar,
Under the stars, who could ask for more?

Crescendo in the Canopy

In the jungle, monkeys sing,
Swinging high, they do their thing.
A parrot squawks in random tones,
While squirrels dance on leafy thrones.

The trees join in with rustling cheer,
As vines become a band right here.
A toucan with a beak so bright,
Hums a tune that feels just right.

But watch out for the sneaky snake,
Who dreams of joining this wild wake.
He strikes a pose, but no one cares,
He's got no rhythm, just some glares.

The show goes on, oh what a sight,
Each creature jiving, feeling light.
In this chaos, peace takes flight,
Nature's comedy, pure delight.

Ephemeral Grace

A butterfly flits, so fancy and free,
With colors that laugh, quite merrily.
But it pauses to sip from a flower's sweet sip,
Then flutters away in a giggling trip.

The daisies lean in for a chat,
While a bee buzzes round, wearing a hat.
They gossip about the blue jay's prance,
As he struts by, in a clumsy dance.

A ladybug lands, quite posh and proud,
Spreading bright joy, like a fluffy cloud.
But the raindrops tumble, and the party is wet,
Still, they laugh on, with no hint of regret.

In moments so brief, they share a fun laugh,
Creating a memory, a whimsical photograph.
Each fleeting encounter brings smiles anew,
In nature's short play, they bid adieu.

Intrigue of Insects

Underneath the leaves, a drama unfolds,
Where ants march in lines, or so I'm told.
A beetle just stares, unsure where to go,
While a grasshopper jokes, always in tow.

The fireflies flicker, like stars on the ground,
As crickets compose in the night all around.
But a wise old spider spins threads of delight,
Sipping dew drops with pure, sweet insight.

"Why hurry?" says one, "Life's like a race!"
But the ladybug grins, "I'm just in the right place."
They plot and they scheme, in their tiny abode,
Creating a buzz, on the bug-laden road.

So gather, dear friends, in this tiny land,
Where fun and mischief go hand in hand.
In the world of the small, laughter is grand,
With each tiny secret, we all understand.

Enigmatic Echoes

In the forest deep, where secrets play,
The muffled giggles bounce and sway.
The owls throw shade at the moonlit show,
While raccoons plot mischief, with snacks in tow.

The echoes dance from tree to tree,
As whispers float on the night breeze free.
A mysterious fox claims he knows it all,
But trips on a twig, with a fumble and fall.

The shadows chuckle at clumsy moves,
As laughter spreads, the night improves.
Fireflies twinkle like stars in the gloom,
Creating a twirl in the darkness' room.

So come join the fun, in the woods where we play,
Each giggle a secret that drifts far away.
In a world where nonsense can never be wrong,
The echoes of joy compose nature's song.

The Voice of the Valley

In the valley where echoes play,
Goats wear headphones, they sway.
Moo's through the speakers, quite loud,
Even the trees look so proud.

The breeze carries tunes of delight,
Bugs on a stage, what a sight!
Crickets are dancing with glee,
A frog joins the band for free.

The sun beams a spotlight so bright,
While squirrels juggle nuts with might.
Each flower giggles in bloom,
Together they banish all gloom.

So raise your glass of sweet tea,
To nature's quirky jamboree!
In this valley, we laugh and unite,
In rhythms of joy, pure and bright.

Fragrant Footsteps

Down the lane, the flowers plot,
With petals painting every spot.
A whiff of trouble, oh dear friend,
Did you really think it would end?

Bees wear tiny hats, so chic,
Buzzing tunes, oh what a peek!
Tulips whisper to daffodils,
Unruly laughter gives us thrills.

Puddles splash with fragrant flair,
Each splash sings songs of spring air.
I tripped on daisies, what a fall,
Just another day, I'll stand tall.

With each step, we dance in glee,
The world's a stage, you see!
Fragrant footsteps lead the way,
In this merry, wild display.

Harvesting Harmonies

On the farm, a tune is born,
Corn sings loudly, it's not worn.
Pumpkins roll, a jovial game,
Chasing each other's funny name.

Scarecrow hums with arms out wide,
Waving sails for the autumn tide.
Chickens cluck like they're in a show,
Fruits join in, all aglow.

The apples gossip, juicy tales,
While carrots dance in leafy veils.
Even the clouds know how to sway,
Harvest time in a playful way.

So gather 'round and take a seat,
Join the harvest, it's quite a feat!
With laughter ripe, the crop will sing,
In the heart of the joy we bring.

Seas of Serenity

On the shore where giggles blend,
Waves tease shells around the bend.
Starfish pose for selfies, bright,
While seagulls squawk in delight.

The tides tickle hearts so deep,
As beach balls make their jumpy leap.
Sandy toes tap to the beat,
Making memories oh-so-sweet.

Dolphins waltz in playful spree,
Splashing water, wild and free.
Even the tidepool throws a dance,
Inviting all to take a chance.

So float your worries with the foam,
Together we'll celebrate home.
In seas of joy, let's make a mark,
With laughter lighting up the dark.

The Language of Leaves

Whispering rustles, a leaf's delight,
Waving hello, it takes flight.
"Hey, branch buddy, look at me!"
Spinning tales in the breeze, so free.

Colors chatter, a gremlin's parade,
Crunching underfoot, an acorn charade.
"Who dropped this?" the forest will tease,
As shadows dance and laughter flees.

Branches gossip, tales of the sun,
Who snagged the sparkle? Was it just fun?
A game of hide-and-seek, don't you see?
Leaves laughing softly, full of glee.

So join the ruckus, plant your sway,
Nature's silly, in its own way.
Come hear the secret, no need to bow,
Just point at the trees and join the row!

A Dance of Dewdrops

Morning giggles on blades of grass,
Dewdrops sparkle, like a glass.
"Catch me if you can," they gleefully hum,
Twirling in circles, oh, what fun!

Sunrise tickles, warmth on the way,
Dewdrops bounce, in a joyful play.
"I'm rolling down, now who's it now?"
Chasing the light, like a clumsy cow.

Each droplet's waltz, a splash of cheer,
Gleeful rounds, let's gather near.
Wiggly, wobbly, they sway and they tilt,
Till sunlight catches, smooth as silk.

So raise a toast, to shimmering scenes,
Dewy giggles, in glittering sheens.
The day's here now, let's join the fun,
With laughter and love, we'll never be done!

Nature's Harmonious Tapestry

Colors collide in a joyful spree,
Nature's palette, wild and free.
Singing colors, oh what a sight,
Bumbling bees with all their might.

Harmonies, a symphony sweet,
The forest applauds with rhythm and beat.
"Look at us jam!" chirps the sparrow,
While squirrels play on their rickety aero.

Bubbles of laughter float high in the air,
As flowers sway with style and flair.
"Plant a seed, it'll sing a tune!"
Bouncing along like a mirthful loon.

So skip through the forest, join the parade,
With nature's band, you'll never fade.
Let's dance with the trees under the sun,
For time spent giggling is joyfully fun!

Syllables of the Season

Whispers of winter, soft and chill,
Snowflakes giggle, an icy thrill.
"Dance with me!" they twirl and slide,
As laughter bounces, a frosty ride.

Spring sings sweet with warm sunny rays,
Flowers shout, "Let's brighten our days!"
Buzzy bees with hats and ties,
Flirting with blooms, oh, what a surprise!

Summer's a riot, sunburned cheer,
Sandcastles rise, no worries here.
"Come splash, come play! Let's soak it in!"
Water fights sparkle, a goofy grin.

Fall's a jester with leaves that parade,
Crunching and swirling, a merry charade.
"Catch 'em if you can!" they flutter about,
With giggling gusts, there's never a doubt!

The Palette of a Poet

In a world of colors bright,
A poet mixes day and night.
With a brush of words he's found,
Painting laughter all around.

He dabs some blue for sad goodbyes,
And slaps a splash of red for lies.
With strokes of yellow, joy unfolds,
In every line, a tale retold.

Green hues for envy, quite the sight,
A swirl of orange brings delight.
The canvas whispers; oh, what fun,
A jolly mess when all is done!

From cheeky rhymes to silly schemes,
His colors spark like funny dreams.
In every verse, a vivid cheer,
The poet's palette brings us near.

Dreaming Among the Boughs

High above where giggles play,
In leafy beds, the squirrels sway.
A dreamer stirs beneath the shade,
As daylight's pranks are gently made.

The birds conspire with a laugh,
To sketch his dreams on nature's path.
A funny tale of falling leaves,
Turns autumn's dance to silly wheeze.

They tickle branches, set them loose,
While acorns drop in endless truce.
As twilight drapes the world in blue,
The dreamer wakes with laughter, too.

"Was it a dream or just a ruse?"
He chuckles meekly, then snores and snooze.
For in that bough, no frown allowed,
Just giggles soft, beneath the cloud.

Rhythms of the Rain

Pitter-patter, what a song,
The rain's a beat where we belong.
With umbrellas flipping in between,
A marching band, a drenching scene.

The raindrops dance on window panes,
A slippery jig of joyous gains.
And puddles form a stage so grand,
Where ducks perform a quacking band.

Splashing boots and squishy shoes,
The rhythm sings of happy blues.
A stomp, a skip, the joy does flow,
As rain creates a funny show.

Each droplet falls with giggles bold,
Painting stories yet untold.
In the world where raindrops reign,
Life's a laugh in every lane!

Blossoming Echoes

In gardens where the flowers speak,
Their whispered jokes give blooms a streak.
Petals giggle, colors shine,
As bees buzz round in funny lines.

The daisies chuckle at the sun,
While tulips tease the morning run.
With every breeze, a tickled scent,
Their playful blooms, a cheerful bent.

"Look at me!" the roses flare,
As bees buzz by without a care.
With every twist and every turn,
Their vibrant voices brightly churn.

So next time when the blossoms play,
Remember laughter leads the way.
In nature's choir, joy freely flows,
In coloring life, as echo grows.

Melodies in a Dewdrop

A tiny pearl upon the grass,
It giggles as the moments pass.
With every splash, a song takes flight,
Tickling toes in morning light.

When puddles wink, the frogs all cheer,
They croak their tunes for all to hear.
The ants parade, a marching band,
Each little foot a tap on land.

A butterfly, with stripes so bold,
Prances by, a sight to behold.
A melody of flaps and gasps,
In nature's choir, the joy it clasps.

So let it rain, let music play,
In dewdrops bright, we'll dance and sway.
With every drop, a laugh we'll share,
In this grand symphony, we're rare.

The Renewal of Radiance

The sun peeks out, with playful rays,
Painting colors in a haze.
The squirrels chase, a comedy,
Right on cue, like props, you see.

A flower yawns, it wakes up slow,
It stretches wide, 'till petals go!
With every breeze, it sways and jives,
Defying norms, it feels alive.

The bees come buzzing, what a show!
Dancing like they stole the glow.
In pollen suits, they spin and twirl,
With buzzing beats, they dance and swirl.

So breathe it in, this goofy light,
Nature's stage, a pure delight.
With every bloom and funny quirk,
We laugh along, it's nature's work.

Whispered Secrets of the Forest

In the woods, where whispers hide,
Trees tell tales, they won't divide.
With branches twirling, secrets sway,
The leaves giggle, come out to play.

A fox in boots struts with a grin,
Proclaims the news, 'Let fun begin!'
The owls wink and chuckle too,
In this grand forest, joy shines through.

Mushrooms wear their polka dots,
They throw a party, connect the spots.
The rabbits hop in silly hops,
Chasing dreams of carrot tops.

So in this grove, where green is wild,
Nature laughs, a playful child.
With every rustle, every cheer,
We hear the forest's jokes so clear.

Chords of the Blossoming Path

Upon the trail where blooms collide,
The petals sing, no need to hide.
Walking along with a silly grin,
Each step a note, let's spin and spin.

The daisies dance, so carefree bright,
Their polka-dot frocks a sheer delight.
With every breeze, a tune they hum,
In this garden, we can't stay glum.

Butterfly flutters, what a show!
It winks and flaps, 'Come on, let's go!'
A chorus of colors, bright and bold,
In nature's band, joy can't be told.

So walk this path, let laughter bloom,
In every step, we make room.
For melodies sweet, and rhythms fast,
A joyous journey, that will last.

Vibrant Verses of the Valley

In a valley where the goats all dance,
A sheep named Larry took a chance.
He wore a hat, set out to sing,
But tripped on grass, oh what a fling!

A cow in shades said, "What a sight!"
She laughed so hard, it felt so right.
The flowers whispered tales so bold,
Of clowns in fields and sheep in gold.

The ants with boots marched in parade,
While caterpillars joined the charade.
A jester frog jumped high with glee,
A pond reflecting pure comedy!

A breeze blew softly, tickled the trees,
As monkeys swung, all buzzing with ease.
In laughter's grasp, the valley shone,
In vibrant hues, they danced 'til dawn!

Echoes of the Emerald Isle

On the Emerald Isle where fairies play,
A leprechaun lost his gold today.
He tripped on clovers, oh what a fall,
And now he's borrowing coins from all!

A fox in flannel sipped Irish tea,
Chuckling at the antics of you and me.
A dance-off started with a jig so bright,
Even the trees swayed with delight!

The rainbows laughed, they twinkled high,
As bardic tales flew through the sky.
With every joke from a feisty hen,
The echoes spread, let's laugh again!

In this land where silliness reigned,
Even the rocks wore smiles unchained.
So raising our cups, let's toast with cheer,
To giggles and whimsy, year after year!

Reflections in Florals

In a garden where the daisies talk,
A dandelion said, "Let's take a walk!"
But with one puff, it blew away,
Now it's a parachute, oh what a day!

Tulips wore sunglasses, looking so cool,
While a busy bee broke every rule.
It danced on petals, doing the twist,
And all the flowers couldn't resist.

Sunflowers stood, with their heads held high,
Making jokes as the clouds floated by.
"Why don't we ever invite the weed?"
"Because it's too wild, that's the rare breed!"

With laughter echoing through the blooms,
The blooms became enchanted rooms.
In a blossom's kiss, humor shines bright,
Reflecting joy from morning to night!

The Woven Tapestry of Earth

On a tapestry made of earth and sun,
A snail raced by, oh, what fun!
With a tiny flag that labeled 'FAST',
It challenged a rabbit, a wild contrast!

The goldfish in ponds wore tiny caps,
Singing songs and laughing with taps.
While squirrels debated over acorn pies,
The trees leaned in with curious sighs.

Bears in pajamas came out to play,
At a tea party held every Wednesday.
With cookies stacked high and jokes to share,
Oh, how a simple laugh filled the air!

In this wacky world where nonsense reigns,
The colors blend, like wild, tangled chains.
Together we weave a silly mirth,
Celebrating joy in the fabric of Earth!

The Symphony of Growth

In the garden, plants play nice,
Worms crawl round, they look like mice.
Every flower has its quirk,
Dancing leaves, a happy smirk.

Tall sunflowers look down with glee,
Laughing at bees, buzzing with spree.
A crooked carrot turns to say,
"You think you're better? Not today!"

Tiny seeds stretch out in rows,
Joking softly, "Here it goes!"
They twist and twirl, can't contain,
It's garden fun, like a prank on grain.

As nature plays its silly score,
We giggle at the zucchini's war.
Fruits and veggies all unite,
For a bouncy, jolly night.

Ode to the Winding Vines

Winding vines with silly hats,
Snaking round like playful cats.
Climbing high to steal the scene,
Whispering secrets, bright and green.

They're tangled up in ancient trees,
Dancing with the buzzing bees.
A grape once said, "Oh dear me,
I'm tripping on this mystery!"

Leaves are giggling, shades of jade,
Droplets fall, oh what a cascade!
"Let's twist and bend, it's vine time fun,
Racing towards the golden sun!"

In the end, a party's flair,
Where every vine is in midair.
Join the hug, let's interlace,
In this wild and playful space.

Whispering Meadows

In meadows green, the grass does tease,
Tickling toes with every breeze.
The daisies, bold, wear silly crowns,
And laugh at birds in fluffy gowns.

A butterfly with fancy wings,
Sings to cows, "Time for some zings!"
While crickets chirp a rhythmic tune,
The goats all dance beneath the moon.

A pond nearby looks quite bemused,
As frogs in ties get quite confused.
They jump and splash, a dance-off spree,
"Who can croak this tune with glee?"

A meadow gala, oh what a sight,
With flowers bright in shared delight.
Each petal flutters, shares a laugh,
In this nature's comedy, let's all quaff.

Enchanted Garden Rhythms

A garden grows with twinkling charms,
Where gnomes do stretch out with their arms.
They sway to beats of rustling leaves,
Juggling with apples, oh, what thieves!

The tulips twist in colored shoes,
Playing hopscotch, sharing views.
"Pick me, pick me!" the blooms all shout,
In this silly place, there's no doubt!

Butterflies are DJs, spinning sounds,
While rabbits hop and dance 'round bounds.
"Just one more turn!" the daisies plead,
This garden's fun is full-speed indeed.

As shadows stretch, the sun bows low,
The garden glows with evening's show.
We laugh and play till stars appear,
In this enchanted space, oh dear!

Tides of Flourishing Fables

In the garden of tales, where flowers wear hats,
Gossipy daisies chatter, while cabbages chat.
Butterflies, in tuxedos, dance with great flair,
While worms hold a party, in soil, unaware.

Tall tales sprout up, like weeds in a patch,
The sunflowers gossip, their heads in a hatch.
With frogs as the jesters, they leap and they croak,
Each flower's a punchline in nature's great joke.

Winds whisper secrets, as petals will sway,
Bumbling bees buzzing, they join in the play.
Each leaf tells a story, in vibrant green tones,
In this merry garden, all plants have their homes.

So come take a stroll through this fabled delight,
Where laughter is blooming, and every leaf's bright.
The tides of this humor are vast and profound,
In the soil of existence, where joy can be found.

The Scented Serenade

In a meadow of laughter, the blooms are a song,
Where roses tell tales that just can't be wrong.
Each petal's a note in the fragrant ballet,
With daisies as dancers, they twirl 'til the day.

Tulips wear perfume, so fragrant and sweet,
While violets strum ukuleles, a treat.
The breeze is a singer, with whispers so light,
As the plants play their symphony, day and night.

Bees gather round for a concert encore,
With pollen confetti, they dance on the floor.
Sunflowers sway, holding hands with the breeze,
Join in this anthem of joy, if you please!

So sing with the flowers, let spirits unite,
In the scented serenade, everything's bright.
With every soft flower, a chuckle, a cheer,
Join this lyrical voyage, there's laughter to hear.

Garden Quatrains

In a garden of giggles, where veggies regale,
A cucumber sings jokes that seldom curtail.
With carrots in hats, and tomatoes in tune,
They throw a big bash under the bright full moon.

The radishes chuckle, their laughter so bold,
While spinach just blushes, its secrets untold.
The peas in their pods whisper fun little quips,
Creating a ruckus with sardonic flips.

The pumpkins bounce stories, like balls with great zest,
While herbs trade off tales, in a comedic fest.
With squash as the star, and chives cheering loud,
This merry green garden attracts a big crowd.

So come to this plot, where the humor is fine,
Each leaf has a jest, each petal a line.
In garden quatrains, together we'll sway,
Laughing with nature, at life's grand buffet.

Flourish and Fable

In the heart of the wood, where stories unfold,
The saplings exchange all the gossip they hold.
With mushrooms as jesters, who giggle and tease,
And squirrels throwing parties, with acorns at ease.

Where vines twist together, creating a scene,
That's tangled in laughter, like a comedy green.
The owls hoot a tune, with witty remarks,
While fireflies giggle and glow in the dark.

With chortles of starlings, the night fills with cheer,
As moonbeams tickle the leaves, drawing near.
This flourishing fable, where whimsy's the game,
Will have you enchanting and never the same.

So wander through pathways where mirth blooms anew,
In a world painted lively, in hues bright and true.
For flourish and fable, hand-in-hand they'll provide,
A riot of laughter, so come down for the ride!

Carried by the Wind

The leaves chime in a dance so bold,
As whispers of stories start to unfold.
A squirrel in a hat, what a sight to see,
Trying to catch a breeze, oh let it be!

The clouds giggle, floating way up high,
While birds wear boots, so they can fly.
A tumbleweed rolls with a wagging tail,
Chasing after dreams on a bright green trail.

A kite gets tangled in a tree's embrace,
The wind just snickers, a cheeky face.
In this breezy frolic, joy is found,
As laughter bubbles, the world spins around.

With every gust, a chorus sings,
Of funny things that breezes bring.
So let's flap and flutter, like leaves in flight,
For life is a jest, and we're here for the light!

Chasing Shadows of the Forest

In the woods, shadows play hide and seek,
A squirrel steals snacks, oh cheeky and sleek.
A deer wearing glasses rounds the bend,
Reading a book, who knew deer could fend?

Beneath swaying oaks, the laughter erupts,
An owl tries to dance, and hilarity erupts.
Mice in tuxedos, all dressed to the nines,
Twist and twirl under the moon's soft signs.

A raccoon with cupcakes gets stuck in a tree,
His friends just giggle, all wild with glee.
They toast with acorns, a feast in the glen,
While shadows weave tales of mischief again.

The night is alive with a mischievous song,
As shadows of fun stretch and belong.
Let's laugh through the night, with critters galore,
In the forest's embrace, life's never a bore!

Reflections in the Rain

Raindrops dance down on the rooftops wide,
Puddles turn mirrors, reflections collide.
A frog with a cape leaps with grand flair,
Jumping for joy in the misty air.

In rubber boots, a cat struts with pride,
Pawprint trails lost in a splashy slide.
While ducks wear bowties, they waddle and quack,
Leaving little ripples, no looking back.

A squirrel thinks twice, then jumps in full glee,
Splashing a rabbit who's sipping sweet tea.
Umbrellas flip over, yes, it's that kind,
As rain brings out laughter that's hard to unwind.

With giggles and grins, the day fades away,
In puddles of joy, the children will play.
So let's catch the raindrops and dance 'til we're sore,
In reflections of laughter, we could ask for no more!

The Pulse of the Prairie

In fields of gold, the wind whispers loud,
A cow wearing shades struts proud in the crowd.
With every soft breeze, the grass starts to sway,
As critters come out for a jazzy display.

A coyote croons with a voice like a bird,
While rabbits tap dance, not one word unheard.
The prairie dogs mingle, in hats they all prance,
Hosting a party, come join the chance!

With daisies as microphones and sun as the stage,
Each creature partakes, they're all filled with gage.
The bison play drums on the ground with a beat,
Creating a rhythm that's truly a treat.

As twilights embrace the vast open space,
The prairie sings boldly, a jubilant place.
In this lively pulse where anything goes,
Let's dance with the prairie and strike a few poses!

Enchanted Grove Melodies

In the grove where laughter flies,
Trees wear hats, oh what a surprise!
Squirrels dance with acorn hats,
While frogs sing tunes for their aristocrat chats.

Breezy whispers, a giggling breeze,
A fox in shades, just trying to tease.
The owls give side-eye, sipping their tea,
As chipmunks juggle for a fee.

Cascading Colors of Spring

The tulips gossip, petals so bright,
Wearing polka dots in morning light.
Butterflies don a fashion parade,
While bees buzz tales of nectar escapade.

Rabbits hop in a conga line,
Singing songs that blend and twine.
Daisies giggle, spotting a prance,
As daisies whisper, "Let's dance, let's dance!"

Sonnet of the Thicket

In tangled weeds, a hedgehog snores,
While hedges chat behind leafy doors.
A deer with glasses, reading the news,
And skunks preparing a scent to amuse.

Bushes giggle, tickling the breeze,
A party sprouting beneath the trees.
Berries wear crowns, feeling so grand,
As butterflies lead the conga band.

Garden of Dreaming Voices

In a garden where whispers bloom,
A sunflower's joke fills the room.
Roses gossip of who's the best,
While lavender hums, taking a rest.

The mushrooms gather for a tea,
Stirring stories of whacky spree.
Violets chuckle, a sweet little band,
Creating melodies across the land.

www.ingramcontent.com/pod-product-compliance
Lightning Source LLC
Chambersburg PA
CBHW072146200426
43209CB00051B/782